Menopause Pink

D0064127

Menopause Pink

Mid-Life Reflections of Wisdom and Humor

Terri Malucci

Published by Creativa Press
2525 Arapahoe Ave., E4 - PMB 548, Boulder, Colorado 80302

Publisher's Cataloging-in-Publication Data
Malucci, Terri
    Menopause pink : mid-life reflections of wisdom and humor /
    edited by Terri Malucci ; graphic design by Li Hertzi. – Boulder, CO:
Creativa Press, 2000
        p. cm.
        ISBN 0-9673744-4-8
    1. Menopause – Miscellanea. I. Malucci, T.

RG186 .M46 2000   99-63720
612.665 – DC21   CIP

Consulting by Christine Testolini, The Integrity Agency, Littleton, CO.

02   01   00   ✱   5   4   3   2   1

Printed in the United States of America

Dedication

*t*o each of you who contributed to this work in any way, you know who you are...

To every one of you who spurred me on by asking, "So, how's that book coming along?"

To every reader, may these words come to you when you need them the most.

Thank You, Great Spirit

for each new day you give to me,
for earth and sky
and sand and sea,
for rainbows
after springtime showers,
autumn leaves
and summer flowers,
winter snowscapes so serene,
harvest field of gold
and green,
beauty shining all around,
lilacs scent
and robins sound,
stars that twinkle high above
and all the people that I love.

Anonymous

Foreword

*a*ll too often women are devalued in our society. Their health issues are poorly researched and they are still treated as second class citizens in the world of commerce. The major life changes of women are typically viewed as "syndromes", diseases, or at the very least, inconveniences that must be tolerated as burdens of womanhood. As a result, women have been cut off from the powerful rhythms and cycles of nature that they personify. Then, after years of menstruation, premenstrual syndromes, medically controlled pregnancies and childbirths, they are told that they are in their final disease, menopause.

Rather than a time of transformation, introspection and spiritual discovery, women in menopause are sold a package of impending doom and death. This debilitating attitude reinforces a brutal scenario of brittle, wilted, sexless women sweating uncontrollably toward their final days.

Terri Malucci speaks from the heart. Her message is timely, lighthearted and heart felt. Menopause can be a new beginning, a time of transformation. Her vision, candor and humor are needed now. Let her lead you laughing on a new journey of self discovery. The power of menopause is anything you allow yourself to make it. The choice is yours!

Dr. Frank Sabatino, D.C. PH.D
Emory University School of Medicine
Atlanta, GA

Menopause
Pink

Be a queen. Be tender. Continue to give birth to new ideas and rejoice in your womanhood...
Oprah Winfrey

Menopause Pink

*i*t all began several weeks before my 47th birthday, with a vision test. I decided it was time to have my eyes checked because I found myself having to sit on my leg while reading restaurant menus or looking at photographs or studying a project at work. To achieve the proper perspective it helped to have more distance between me and the page. By tucking my leg under my seat I had a built-in concealed booster chair. At the grocery store I squinted, honing in on those tiny directory listings and aisle numbers.

Once I asked my boss at a meeting what it meant when your arms aren't long enough or you aren't tall enough to see what is before you. He replied, "It means you're at that age...you probably need bifocals. They make glasses for that, you know."

So, off to the vision clinic. Dr. Day, a rather humorless man, carefully examined my eyes then recommended a "Progressive" lens and sent me out to the showroom to select frames. A woman offered me a chair and said, "Are these your first trifocals? Have you ever worn bifocals?"

Trifocals! For me? Surely she had the wrong person. No, she meant me, and she meant trifocals. Then I remembered a Peanuts cartoon about someone dreading getting older and having to get those "bifocal teeth". Here we go, the downward slide.

Several weeks later, just before *The Birthday*, I picked up my new glasses. After being instructed to get into the habit of pointing my nose directly at what I wanted to look at, I went to the car. I wanted to look at the keyhole to unlock the door. Step back, point nose, arms aren't long enough. Drive, point nose at speedometer, look ahead, point nose, look in rear view mirror. Point nose. Lots of neck action.

Park car. Take a walk along the pedestrian mall to practice. Toe of sandal scrapes curb. Misjudge curb height. Plop foot down loudly on sidewalk. Run into newspaper stand. I was pointing my nose at the curb when I should have been looking up.

Go to coffee shop. Point nose up at wall menu. Order latte. Stick nose in purse to locate wallet. College student at counter asks me if I'm all right. (He thinks maybe I'm drunk.)

Balancing my coffee cup and purse, I try to walk unobtrusively to a table outdoors to sip along, focus, and read the paper while I get used to these damn things and wait for my boyfriend to join me. When he arrives he sweetly compliments me on my new look. He agrees to walk me down the mall, just for practice. Plop, plop. You can hear us coming. Steve gently announces, "OK, step down. Curb. Step up." He's four years younger than I am and I think he's humoring me. I stop at each cross street, wagging my head back and forth like one of those stuffed dogs you can put in the back window of your car. Ones with red dot light bulb eyes. You've seen them.

With resolve I force myself to practice wearing my glasses "all of the time." While carrying groceries up three flights to my front door, I fall up the stairs. I bruise my shin and curse the stupidity of me.

More subtle signs that summer. Meeting my friend, Maureen, for lunch and listening to her praise the virtues of elastic waist bands in jeans. Of how she was on her way to a meeting one afternoon, became disoriented while trying to find a parking place, and sat in her car weeping. Somehow our conversations have turned from relationship issues, work, and our friends, to feeling fat, lifting weights and getting fatter, and how she cries at the smallest little things.

I add that I think my dryer is on the blink because my clothes seem to be shrinking all at once. Even my underpants are uniformly too tight. She says, "Try pants with elastic, they don't seem to shrink as much." Right.

I meet another friend for coffee. We sit outdoors on a perfect summer morning. I begin to sweat. She glows serenely in her crisp Size 2 linen dress. We're engrossed in a marathon girl talk session. It is my turn to speak. Mid-sentence I go blank, totally blank. Words I have planned to speak escape me. "Forgive me, Gayla, but my mind is empty. What was I saying? I'm so warm right now, I just need to sit very still for a minute."

She smiles and gently says, "It's OK. Do you think you could possibly be starting menopause?"

"Me? Oh, no, I don't think so. I'm just so stressed out. And it's been so hot this summer. I think I'm just tired." Um o-tay.

"I'm really OTAY," I say again.

Well, I'm not OK. I'm embarrassed. Where did those jumblewords come from? On my way home I think that maybe I've had a small stroke. Just a tiny one. It'll be my own little secret.

Later, near the end of August, Steve and I fly to San Francisco for the weekend. In the airplane my body begins to swell. It's just so damn hot, record heat in the city. My watchband is so tight that it cuts a ridge into my wrist. Even my earrings feel too tight.

We take to the streets to explore. It's crowded, people jostling me on the sidewalk. Inside my head I'm screaming, "The next person who bumps into me is going to get his lights punched out!" Steve tries to hold my hand. I stop walking and snap at him. "Don't, don't touch me. It's too hot."

Nothing fits. I can't get my jeans zipped. My panty hose creep and itch. My skin is crawling. I eat just a lettuce salad for dinner, hoping to shrink by morning so I won't have to go around naked.

While getting ready for bed, my stomach, suddenly free from confines of clothing, grows. And grows. It spreads into a doughy mass. I go to the bed, sit down next to Steve and say, "I have something to show you. I think something is wrong with me. Look at this. I pull my gown snugly across my protruding abdomen. There is a giant belly sitting on my lap! I poke it with my index finger. "Look at this," I demand. "What is happening to me?"

I feel that it is only fair to tell him what's going on so that he won't try to come near me. I am ashamed. I feel fat and ugly and guilty at what I am becoming. I blame myself for letting myself go. For not doing enough situps, not eating lettuce for more meals, for not taking care of myself.

I've always had to watch my weight, always beaten myself up over it, and been severely depressed by my body. Suddenly I realize how vain I've been. How being attractive, smart and moderately successful have been givens. Taken for granted. You don't know what you have until it's gone. My body is not cooperating for some reason. I'm cultivating Ethel Merman arms, jellified thighs, a little ridge of flesh above my bra, and, oh, let's not forget that stomach!

So, the year passes. I am at a trade show walking toward my booth. I can't remember what city I'm in. Then I panic. When I find my place, I ask Steve what city we're in. He thinks I'm teasing him. When he realizes that I'm sincere, he looks stunned.

I'm at a business meeting. It's my turn to speak. I can't. I'm stressed out, go blank, and put my head in my hands. My colleagues look worried as I leave work early. I believe that I've had another one of those small strokes.

I call my doctor and describe symptoms. He diagnoses over the phone. "Water retention. Take these pills, and take one of the little blue ones when you feel a little crazy and tense. They'll take the edge off. It's just PMS. Don't worry."

I take the pills, starve myself, binge, feel guilty, flabby, crabby, hot, tired, and sexless. I wake up in a pool of sweat, hair soaking wet, little puddles beneath me, streams running down my cleavage and the inside of my arms. I get up, change night gowns and conclude to myself that "I must be coming down with something."

I miss my period. Then I get two in two weeks. Join Weight Watchers. Follow the plan religiously. Start going to the gym. Gain 2 pounds. Fast for a day in hopes of getting into my work clothes. Get another period. Lose .02 pounds. The scale lady tells me to hang in there. So I hang. My breasts hang. Sweat collects underneath them. My thighs rub together. Everything is just too tight. What is happening to me?

And so it goes. Quiet signals, gentle and not so gentle signs. Ignored and rationalized away into a deep cavern of denial. Maybe I just need a vacation.

At work we change health insurance plans and I must select a new physician. I choose a woman doctor. Time to start anew, clear the deck, turn myself in, come clean. Dr. Offner entered the examining room and asked me what was up. On a scrap of newspaper I'd quickly jotted down a laundry list of what was bothering me. Here it is:

- ✽ no period
- ✽ toothache pain in left side
- ✽ sore breasts
- ✽ weight up and down and up
- ✽ feel like I'm always on a treadmill
- ✽ depressed
- ✽ tired
- ✽ stressed
- ✽ no sexual interest

✽ overwhelming feeling of despair about death of parents, even though they're still alive

As I read it to her line by line in quick succession, she slowly nods her head. "Let's do blood work, an exam, and see where we are." I begin to sob. "And here's what else is bothering me. My parents have become my children. My mom has brain damage and needs my dad's constant care. He won't make a will and if something happens to him, I mean, *when* something happens to him, I will gladly care for her. But all of his important papers are written on backs of envelopes and kept in his horrendously messy desk drawers. He says I'll know what to do when the time comes."

Dr. Offner delicately interjects, "Is there any possibility that you are pregnant?" Hah! It's June and I haven't had sex yet this year. My boyfriend says that I'm a roller coaster and leaves me alone while he tries to discover what "set me off" this time.

At times I speak emotionally, passionately, about how I feel about life. It's passing me by. I begin many sentences with, "Before I die I want to see the world...I want to travel, to run away from home...I want...I want...I want to stop feeling sad and crabby."

After handing me a Kleenex, the doctor asks my age, and when my mother went through menopause. I don't know, we've never talked about it.

"Well, you certainly exhibit several symptoms. Have you had any hot flashes? How are your periods? Let's do some tests and you come back to see me in another week." I have an ultrasound at the hospital. A week of waiting. What if? What if this little pain in my side is a tumor? What if I have cancer? Remember Gilda Radner? She just got ovarian cancer and died? Just like that! Poof...she was gone. If it could happen to her, it could happen to me. I was expecting the worst but hoping for the best when I went back for test results. Dr. Offner opened my file and wheeled her little stool closer to me. "Tests tell us that you are peri-menopausal. Your blood work reveals marked change in hormone levels and you're at the beginning. There's also an ovarian cyst that we'll check again in two months. In the meantime, you may want to read *The Silent Passage*. It's very good." Then she gave me a sheet describing HRT — that's short for Hormone Replacement Therapy. "You can think about it. Let's see how the hot flashes are going, too." She wrote me a prescription for a vacation and sent me on my way.

I walk to the car in shock. How can this be happening to me already? I'm not ready to do this. How will I tell Steve? I just need a little time to get used to this. I feel like I did when I got my first period in 5th grade. It's just too soon.

I go to the library and check out *The Silent Passage*. It helps. Then I read like a demon. Everything I can find, including *The New Our Bodies, Ourselves*. They write about me in Chapter V entitled WOMEN GROWING OLDER. I'm a classic case. No, it wasn't a series of small strokes. Or cancer. Or insanity. It's just menopause.

It is several weeks later. I feel so much better in my head because it's all relative. Another part of life, a part of me. I can almost see the humor in all of this. Which brings me to the point of why I put this book together.

During my search for information about this new phase of life, I found a plethora of serious, albeit necessary, books. For example, in 1777, a certain John Leak wrote in *Chronic or Slow Diseases Peculiar to Women*, "These include pain and giddiness of the head, hysteric disorders, and a midlife female weakness." His colleague wrote that "A large percentage of women acquire a vapid cowlike feeling called a "negative state." Other titles like *Managing Your Menopause* abound with glossaries of clinical terms, drawings of pre-menopausal healthy ovaries vs. shrunken ovaries. Many overused negative words like risk, disease, deterioration, and atrophy. One female Freudian disciple even referred to menopause as a woman's "partial death."

I couldn't find a book that helped me feel better. Then one night while having dinner with my mother and 96-year-old grandmother, I began quizzing them about what menopause was like for them. Mom said to her mom, "You never had any symptoms, did you? We never saw you sweat or anything." "Oh, boy," she replied. "One summer I was driving to California. Everyone else was asleep in the back seat, but I remember looking in the rear view mirror to make sure my hair wasn't on fire. I never said a word about it to anybody because we just didn't talk about it.

Not even to our doctors or our best friends. Instead, we made vague comments about the warm weather, glowed and glistened with perspiration, and changed the subject."

After this encounter, I began collecting stories from everyone I met, from anyone who seemed interested in talking or writing about their experiences and memories about this time of our lives. And do you know what? There is lightness, hope and humor about this wonderful second chance at life. It puts it all in perspective when elderly ladies can't remember much about it, mostly because people just didn't talk about such things. And because it happened so long ago that whatever went on has become a rather distant memory.

Here are their stories, thoughts, and feelings. Some shared a favorite poem, wrote a few lines, or created an expression. May their words bring joy, smiles, and hope to you, my sisters young and old.

Menopause Pink

The Stories

Suzanne

*m*enopause...this is a somewhat perplexing topic. I never really wanted to think about it at all, so I took a "head in the sand" position. Menopause being a fact of life, however, it is difficult, nay impossible, to ignore forever. We are told it is a natural progression of life, one of those many changes we must accept but are really never ready to face. Change is constant and inevitable, so why are we so reluctant?

To preface my story, I must tell you that I am a caterer. And as anyone who's ever done this type of work knows, it is demanding and the hours are long. When I'm really busy it is common to begin the day around 4 a.m. Needless to say, I am alone in my kitchen at that hour. Often I throw on my sweats and run to work without much thought about properly dressing for the day. Usually I have on sweats and nothing else!

It happened one cold winter's morning in December. I was in the kitchen very early and for no known reason I was crying. I couldn't stop no matter what. I rationalized that it was just a very busy time and stress was taking its toll. Suddenly I was burning up! I was so hot I couldn't stand it. I realized that if I shed my sweats I would be totally naked and this would not be in keeping with health department guidelines for commercial kitchens. With sweat running down my chest, I did the only thing I could...shed the sweats and wrapped myself in aprons. What a sight I must have been! The aprons, of course, didn't cover everything, and me with tears streaming down my face, trying desperately to keep cooking!

This was my very first experience with those devilish power surges and is a favorite memory of my passing into this new phase of life.

Never eat more than you can lift.
Miss Piggy

Gwendolyn

*W*e need to share our stories, to gain knowledge from one another. Our ancestors taught us to share our rite of passage into womanhood so that we all become empowered in the process. A Kenyan proverb declares, "Talking with one another is loving one another." My mother walked me through the transitions of womanhood before she died. She gave me monthly reports about her "pause" because she wanted me to be ready for my own. Knowing what's to come helps keep us composed, confident and emotionally prepared for the changes and challenges of menopause.

By the year 2000, nearly one third of American women will be over 50. But "over 50" does not mean "over the hill" or scatterbrained or in the throes of a hot flash. It means that, finally, you're in the driver's seat, fully in charge of your life and unencumbered by the fear associated with lack of knowledge about the changes that are happening to you.

Remember, menopause is the pause that can renew, transform, revitalize and create a new you. The "change" is not the beginning of the end; it's the beginning of a new beginning. The best is yet to come.

We're the elders of the tribe, and the elders are charged with the tribe's survival and well being.
Maggie Kuhn

Bonnie

*W*hen I was in 10th grade, I went to the bathroom and could not believe that I was bleeding! I knew nothing of a monthly period and all of that blood was so frightening. My girlfriend explained what was happening. That night I told my mother about how confused I felt and that I found out about being a woman the hard way. She said, "We don't talk about those things."

After a hysterectomy in 1975, I never took any pills. Never had any hot flushes, either. Now, at 72, I doubt that I ever will. Talk about menopause...it was menostop for me.

I think a woman's cycle is what she makes it. I never remember my mom or any of my sisters having any problems. Maybe we were an unusual family. One thing we did have was lots of love.

Eudelle

*t*hroughout my life as a mother and wife, I continued to socialize with a group of women who had stayed together from kindergarten on. Once a month we'd gather at one of our homes for a Friday night game of pinnocle, conversation, and dessert. As the years passed, talk evolved from high school graduation, becoming war time brides, our husbands returning from overseas during the war, to subsequent children resulting from those reunions. Then came the giggling and wonderment about how our mothers were going through the change. Although they never admitted to it, they were changing. And we noticed how they seemed to be wearing that certain shade of pink. Closets overflowing with Hot Pink! We named it *Menopause Pink* and the term became synonymous with being in *The Change of Life*. And with being hot.

This is Menopause Pink:

The heyday of a woman's life is the shady side of fifty.
Elizabeth Cady Stanton

Donna

*t*he only thing I can say about menopause is...Have a hysterectomy!

Select a doctor your own age so that
you can grow old together.
H. Jackson Brown, Jr.

Linda

Passage

I was all set
To write about the last flicker
Of a dying flame.

But endings presage beginnings
So
Relight the fire!
The past kindles the future.

A small, warm glow at least--
Maybe a roaring flame,
Or something between--
Life.

June

My advice is, "Don't go through menopause unless absolutely necessary!" However, if you do find yourself in the midst of the middle, don't hesitate to go to a specialist to help you through the hot, dry spots, if you know what I mean!

...all events are blessings given to us to learn from.
Elizabeth Kubler-Ross

Phyllis

I wonder what I will be like when all of this is over.

❀

Will I still be me?

❀

Will I look different?

❀

Will I be wiser?

❀

*i*t is more stunning than I expected, mostly because I never expected it. When we get our periods we're too young to know what is before us. We have our mothers to tell us how to be young ladies. When we say goodbye to our periods we are aware enough to know that this phase doesn't seem so exciting and filled with dreams yet to be fulfilled, of husbands and babies. This is different. Subconsciously during the night I feel that my period has started and get up to furtively check. No, must just be a gas pain. Nothing there. It takes a minute to tell myself, "Oh, yeah, I'm in menopause, I don't do that any more. Oh yeah, in a month I'll be 50. How'd that happen? I don't feel 50. Oh, yeah! No more periods, no more birth control, no more monthly insanity. Oh YES!"

Growth is exciting; growth is dynamic and alarming.
Vita Sackville-West

Sarah

i was born knowing how to spell. It's just one of those things. Suddenly when I sat down to write a letter or a grocery list, I didn't know how to spell the simplest words, like "lettuce" and "sure." Then I finally realized what was happening to me. Fuzzy brain syndrome! I know when this hormone volleyball is over and my body is balanced once again, I will be able to spell again. But for now I prefer to call this stage Mental Pause.

Anonymous was a woman.
Anonymous

E-mail - Fill In the Blanks Menopause Self-Test

Which of the symptoms below belongs to each statement?

_____1. You sell your home heating system at a garage sale.

_____2. The person you sleep with complains about snow piling up on the bed.

_____3. Your husband jokes that instead of buying a wood stove, he'll just use you to heat the family room this winter. Rather than saying you are not amused, you shoot him.

_____4. You write your kid's names on Post-It notes.

_____5. Your husband chirps, "Hi, Honey, I'm home," and you reply, "Well, if it isn't Ozzie F--- ing Nelson."

_____6. You change underwear after every sneeze.

_____7. The phenobarbitol dose that wiped out the Heaven's Gate cult gives you four hours of decent, uninterrupted rest.

_____8. You find guacamole in your hair after a Mexican dinner.

_____9. You need Jaws of Life to help you out of the car after eating at an Italian restaurant.

_____10. You think Antonio Banderas is, "OK, I guess."

_____11. You ask Jiffy Lube to put you up on a hoist.

_____12. You're on so much estrogen, you take the Brownie troop on a field trip to see the Chippendales.

Menopause Symptoms:

A. Libido Loss

B. Hot Flashes

C. Sudden Weight Gain

D. Mood Swings

E. Nightsweats

F. Mild Incontinence

G. Irritability

H. Fatigue

I. Sleeplessness

J. Dryness

K. Hormone Therapy

L. Memory Loss

Answers: 1B, 2E, 3D, 4L, 5G, 6F, 7I, 8H, 9C, 10A, 11J, and 12K.

Myra

*i*never knew it was possible to sweat in the shower. It is also possible to go an entire Colorado winter without ever wearing a coat. Everyone thinks you're crazy. You know things are heating up biologically when you drive to Christmas Eve dinner with the air conditioner on and you'd put the top down on your convertible if you could. If it weren't for the howling wind and snow flurries.

It's sad to grow old, but nice to ripen.
Brigitte Bardot

Gladys

*m*enopause happened to me 20 years ago with very few problems. It was just another phase in my life. I was one of the rare people who never took any hormones or therapy of any kind.

Twelve Basic Principles
of the Utian Program

1. You can live better and longer.
2. Illness and disability are not inevitable in the later years.
3. It is within your power to be healthy and vibrant.
4. You are important, you are wanted, and you are needed.
5. Appreciate your additional experience.
6. Repay your debt to yourself.
7. You are as old as you allow yourself to feel.
8. Time flies--each day really is a once-in-a-lifetime opportunity.
9. If you have money, spend it on yourself.
10. Ignore societal attitudes that are outdated.
11. Enjoyment of life is not sinful or self-indulgent.
12. You can control your destiny.

Menopositive!
Kathleen Marie Seivert

Alvira

menopause was a delight--my last menstruation was when I was in Paris.

I do have a question, though. Why is it that Menopause, Menstrual, Menstruate, and Menstruation all begin with MEN? That's probably why some women get depressed during MENopause or go a little MENtal!

I also remember hot flashes so intense that my nail polish got tacky!

The change of life is a time of release when a woman begins to reap the benefits of all that she has learned and done.
Lynn V. Andrews

Germaine

*W*omen over fifty already form one of the largest groups in the population structure of the western world. As long as they like themselves, they will not be an oppressed minority. In order to like themselves they must reject trivialization by others of who and what they are. A grown woman should not have to masquerade as a girl in order to remain in the land of the living.

The snow goose need not bathe to make itself white. Neither need you do anything but be yourself.
Lao-Tse

Patricia

i am noticing a great increase in my creative thoughts. My eyes want to use a camera again. I long to write and photograph the world with a new vision.

We have a second chance in postmenopause...to focus on the thing we most love and redirect our creativity in the most individual of ways.
Gail Sheehy

Leslie

*m*enopause is the time when women become smarter with their lives. I look at us as women of wisdom. Those blessed hot flashes are just your body's way of making you aware of your aliveness.

It is a time of rejuvenation and inspiration. I am filled with positive thoughts about one phase of my life closing and another opening. It is time of honoring oneself after child-birth and nurturing others. All of these feelings encompass wisdom.

Like an ability or a muscle, hearing your inner wisdom is strengthened by doing it.
Robbie Gass

Ann

i loved menopause because it meant no more periods. I welcomed those hot flashes. I just wore less silk!

Moods, like fashions, come and go. Wear something comfortable.
Calendar Wisdom

Sylvia

*i*n December of 1997 I went to visit my mother. She noticed my body had changed. Her words to me: "Are you pregnant?" I looked at her and gave a hearty laugh and said, "NO!" Her words to me..."Well, maybe you are. Your butt is bigger, your breasts rounder, your legs are also bigger!" At that point I told my mother, "Something is happening to me." I told her that I haven't seen my period for four months. "What?" she said. I said, "That's right." She asked me if I'd seen the doctor and I told her I was planning to when I got back to New York. By the way, my mother lives in North Carolina. She was so shocked to see that my body had changed so suddenly, and so was I.

The symptoms that I experienced after I left my mother were hot flashes, hot and cold sweats, swollen hands and feet, water retention, nausea, fatigue, and a terrible taste in my mouth. I had also been eating things that I wouldn't normally go near. In short, I thought my body was going to bust open. I made an appointment with a doctor. He gave me a thorough examination, only to prescribe me Premarin. What happened to me while taking it was horrible. I lost control. This was not funny anymore. My body was ready to change, but not my mind.

I haven't seen my period since December. When I travel a lot, I'm always taking sanitary napkins. Not anymore. The stage I was going through was a sudden shock to me. I have seen people grow older and change by appearance drastically and that's one thing I will fight forever. My younger brother, Melvin, who is with me in spirit, often reminded me about staying in shape and forever looking young. Now, I know that is possible. A lot has to do with state of mind, and we know that the mind is a powerful tool. I am adjusting to this new body of mine. I have no choice, but we can control some of the things that happen to us. I guess I will always be young at heart.

Mardi

*m*enopause is a major transition affecting your entire body and every system in it. Frequently in Western society this transition puts us out of balance due to high stress, pollution, or inadequate diet. In my work as a nurse practitioner, I emphasize diet and exercise as ways to regain balance. Our society does not give women room to make this transition, so they must "make room for themselves."

Every woman goes through a different menopause, because each body has been differently influenced over the last 40 or 50 years. I've discovered that this is a time of re-birthing when you, too, may revisit health and emotional issues you've experienced up to this point. I know it sounds scary, but if you look at menopause as a second chance to resolve these matters, you'll come out the other side of this transition to a true Power Surge. This is your passage into the wise woman years. There is nothing as beautiful, strong and interesting as a woman over 40!

I teach a class called "Cooking for the Wise Woman: Recipes for Menopause", in which we learn to incorporate ingredients rich in phytoestrogens like soy and flaxseed into our diets. For example, if you eat soy even once a day, you'll help yourself avoid the worst of the hot flashes. Here's a bit of inspiration from my recipe collection, a fun dessert that none of us should eat too regularly!

Bailey's Irish Creme Chocolate Mousse

1/2 cup frozen white grape juice
1 16 oz. cake soft silken tofu
4 Tbsp. unsweetened cocoa
3 Tbsp. Bailey's Irish Creme Liquor
1/2 tsp. salt
4 Tbsp. raw sugar
1 Tbsp. vanilla
1 Tbsp. maple syrup
1 envelope unflavored gelatin or agar agar

Put gelatin in cold grape juice to dissolve. Heat; stir to prevent lumps. Place tofu, cocoa, salt, raw sugar, and maple syrup in food processor. Blend till very smooth. Add gelatin mixture, vanilla, and Irish Creme. Blend. Adjust flavor by adding more sugar, cocoa, or liquor. Put in individual glasses and refrigerate 2 hours or until set. Garnish with chocolate shavings. Serves 4.

Valerie

"*i*t's almost like the gay community has shown us the way. We're coming out of the closet about a natural function. It's not like our mother's and grandmother's attitudes toward menopause. We're not whispering."

The Denver Post

What would I do today if I were brave?
Jana Stanfield

Madeline

i know the perfect antidote for menopause! Get pregnant when you're 39...it makes you young all over again. I went merrily along until age 53 when I just stopped menstruating with no problems, no hot flashes, so I say I never went through *The Change*. Even my doctor said he'd never had anyone go through so easily.

Life is a series of natural and spontaneous changes.
Lao-Tse

Elizabeth

Ode to be in April Now that September's Here

My PMS has fled the scene
Hot Flashes cease to be
My figure isn't quite so lean
I'm now a chubby me.

I bravely wave good-bye to youth
Embrace my many flaws
And down a slug of sweet Vermouth
I'm deep in menopause.

If you're pushing 50, that's exercise enough.
Bumper Sticker Wisdom

Annette

i finally got around to talking to the people I know at the Senior Center and hospital about what they remember about menopause. I must report that we're a boring lot. Most said it was so long ago, that in retrospect it didn't amount to much. Peggy said there were days when she could time hot flashes by her watch, every 40 minutes.

That's about it.

We in middle age require adventure.
Amanda Cross

Erma

beloved humorist and syndicated columnist Erma Bombeck recalled asking her mother the meaning of menopause. Her rather unclinical response was, "It's when your baby basket dries up."

Erma then asked if this time of life was anything to worry about and her mother reassured her. "Only if you hate dry skin, migraines, itching, palpitations, hot flashes, sweats, depression, apprehension, nervousness, insomnia, and crawling sensations under your skin."

Her grandmother added her two cents worth, when unable to actually say Menopause, she said, "Maybe you're going through the you-know-what."

Have faith, dearheart. You'll get through it.
Mom

Rose

*d*uring my first hot flashes I'd panic and fight them. Then the more I read about menopause, the more I understood that my entire physiology was readjusting. I developed these Hot Flash Coping Strategies:

Calm down and acknowledge that your body needs to perspire, install a ceiling fan in your bedroom, eat popsicles in the middle of the night, wear cotton night gowns, and learn to accessorize with bandanas and neck scarves. (They catch the sweat before it runs down your shirt.) If you begin flashing while grocery shopping, head immediately to the frozen food aisle, open the cooler, and proceed to read ice cream carton labels for fat content until the flash passes.

> *Hope is the feeling you have that*
> *the feeling you have isn't permanent.*
> Jean Kerr

Roberta

a friend mailed me this story: A woman went to her doctor. "You've got to help me! Every time I go to the bathroom, dimes come out!" The doctor told her to go home, relax with her feet up, and come back in a week.

The next week she kept her appointment. "It's gotten worse, doctor! Now every time I go to the bathroom, quarters come out!" Again she is directed to rest and return in one week.

Week three arrives and the woman yells, "Doctor, I'm still not any better! Every time I go to the bathroom, Susan B. Anthony dollars come out! What is wrong with me?"

The doctor smiles and delivers his diagnosis. "Relax, you're just going through your change."

Joan

*W*e all can use the challenges of the menopausal metamorphosis as motivators to enter a new relationship with our bodies, minds, and energy systems. The gift of this middle cycle of midlife can be a vital and healthy lifestyle that not only helps protect us against many of the degenerative diseases that accompany aging, but also gives us the energy to use our wisdom to make this world a better place.

The longer I live, the more beautiful life becomes.
Frank Lloyd Wright

Peggy

When I Am An Old Woman

I shall wear purple
With a red hat which doesn't go, and doesn't suit me.
And I shall spend my pension on brandy and summer gloves
And satin sandals. And say we've no money for butter.
I shall sit down on the pavement when I'm tired
And gobble up samples in shops and press alarm bells
And run my stick along the public railings
And make up for the sobriety of my youth.
I shall go out in my slippers in the rain
And pick the flowers in other people's gardens
And learn to spit.
You can wear terrible shirts and grow more fat.
And eat three pounds of sausage at a go
Or only bread and a pickle for a week.

And hoard pens and pencils and beermats and things in boxes.
But now we must have clothes that keep us dry
And pay our rent and not swear in the street
And set a good example for the children.
We will have friends to dinner and read the papers.
But maybe I ought to practice a little now?
So people who know me are not too shocked and surprised
When suddenly I am old and start to wear purple.

From *Warning* by Jenny Joseph

*There is no greater power in the world than the zest
of a postmenopausal woman.*
Margaret Mead

Veronica

*W*hen I heard I was beginning menopause I decided to buy myself diamond earrings, great big ones, as a present to brighten up my face.

I also gave myself permission to let go...to acknowledge that the time I've been working and saving for is NOW. Instead of being so frugal with myself, I'm buying little presents for me. Nothing major, just a new shampoo, foot massage cream, a CD, a magazine here and there. Little indulgences, like going to the movies during the day. Being more selective about who I spend time with. And clearing my physical surroundings of clutter.

I've also started reading obituaries and keeping a mental tally of death ages. Plenty of people, younger than I am, are cashing in their chips for one reason or another. I pepper my meaningful conversations with examples. "But, you see, I was reading the obits this morning and a 39-year-old woman died of breast cancer...that could be me...let's go on vacation! I dare you!" I could be the one gone, in just a few years. Come on, let's get with it! There is a sudden urgency in my pleas.

This is a time for reassessing values. For letting go and being ultimately generous with myself and others. It is good. It is liberating. To act instead of dream is so energizing. To be centered, self-aware and kind to oneself is comforting. To be work in progress is very satisfying!

You will have a very pleasant experience.
Fortune Cookie Wisdom

Marie

by the time we hit fifty, we have learned our hardest lessons. We have found out that only a few things are really important. We have learned to take life seriously, but never ourselves.

You can only perceive real beauty in a person as they get older.
Anouk Aimee

Jan

*m*y attitude is much different from when I was younger. I needed to have a hysterectomy and felt very positive about my decision to have this controversial operation. Why not take out the parts that you aren't using and no longer need?

This was my first experience with a female gynecologist and surgeon. It was just great!

To keep the body in good health is a duty...otherwise we shall not be able to keep our mind strong and clear.
Buddha

Ruth

*a*s for the menopause, I didn't know it happened. The scant bits I recall rather tell me that I was relatively late, i.e., 55 or older. As far as any thought of losing anything, I counted it a plus—no more investment in Kotex, I had no hot flashes, no depression or mania, no weight change. My explanation for all this is — I was at the height of my career, doing things I loved, had a solid marriage, went to Europe every year, and therefore, missed the show!

Since I am a physician, one aspect of post-menopause about which I do want to make a statement concerns the possibility of osteoporosis. Certain women with a family history of this malady who are small in stature and inactive may find it wise to use hormone therapy. My family history is positive, my stature is what most of us call small, but I am not inactive. I have been regularly in an exercise program since 1969 and at this time do aerobic exercise three to five times a week. I do not partake of the senior offerings. Instead, I participate in a class with college-aged men and women. I am also on oral progesterone and transdermal estrogen. When I want to visit my grandchildren and great-grandchildren, I get in my car and drive to Texas, the Western Slope of Colorado or the far northwest in the Seattle area.

Life can be very interesting, can it not? There are times when I think we go in circles and find it difficult to know where we have been.

Do not weep. Do not wax indignant. Understand.
Spinoza

Fern

*m*y fond memory of the change of life was freedom from pain during the monthly period.

At my club meeting so many of the ladies would sit and fan themselves. Their faces would flush, because there was no air conditioning back then.

Is it hot in here, or is it me?
G. Sand

Judith

*t*his is a time to stop and reflect on all we've accomplished and created so far. We no longer need to crash from one phase to another, trying to find out who we are and where we belong. We can now give more fully to our wider communities.

Get involved with something bigger than yourself.
Dick Burdette

Jeanne

i am one of the fortunate ones who breezed through this period very easily and had a family who made it so. Health wise I think taking vitamin B complex eases the nerves and calms you...keeps you from yelling or getting upset with the teenagers in your life or happenings at that time.

Personally, I think the most important thing is to work part-time and keep busy so you do not have time for depression and for feeling sorry that time has slipped by so quickly.

Life after this period is so great without having to worry or plan things around "That Time of the Month."

In our group we call it Menopause Purple. This goes with

the graying of our hair and purple being a great color to wear. I have had friends who take this seriously and won't ever wear purple again!

I believe in hard work. It keeps the wrinkles out of the mind and the spirit.
Helena Rubinstein

Li

Make us whole and wise, Sweet Angel Goddess, so that we may awaken, nurture and love freely and fully.

Loretta

Yesterday, at the end of tap dancing class, I brought up the subject of menopause to my fellow students.

Steve, our token male, said, "Hell, my ex-wife's been through it. My girlfriend's going through it. And the best story I've ever heard about it was this:

A female tourist vacationing in California began having some health problems. She went to a local doctor who listened to her complaints, then asked. "Have you been through the menopause?" The woman replied, "Omigosh, no! We haven't even seen Disneyland yet!"

We are all here for a spell, get all the good laughs you can.
Will Rogers

Lucita

*L*ucita was an extraordinary teacher who's special interest was women's health issues at mid-life. She inspired us with her devotion to physical fitness and spiritual quests. During the last year of her life, even though her brain cancer had so rudely escaped from remission, Lucy taught us special lessons from her hospital bed in the nursing home. A group of us went to keep her company one evening. As we left, she called out, "Remember, you're all goddesses!"

"Creating Personal Moments of Joy" was a workshop Lucy taught. Her message to each of us was to believe in ourselves and to remain active throughout all the days of our lives. She knew what she was talking about, for she became a champion body builder after her 50th birthday. After brain surgery. Not too many of us will begin weight training at this stage of the game; but we can chase our own rainbows and remember our rose, Lucy. From her notebook:

The Moment of Power Is Now

You can change your reality
The moment of power is now
Trust your inner authority
The moment of power is now
Power goes with integrity
The moment of power is now
We have a date with destiny
The moment of power is now
Make the choice to be all you can
The moment of power is now
Take a stand while you still can
The moment of power is now.

Mary T

*a*fter having eight kids and numerous miscarriages in between, my mother seemed unflappable. She never swore and went to Mass daily. One day I came home from school and I heard Mom cursing to herself behind the bathroom door. In a chant she repeated, "Shit, shit, shit."

"Ma, what's the matter? Are you all right?"

She replied, "No, I'm not all right! Here I am over 50. I thought I was done with this, and now I've got a period. That's what's the matter!"

I never trust anyone who won't say "shit".
Fanny Bryce

Florence

going through menopause was easy for me as falling off a log -- it was suffering through the endless five or seven days of bleeding so profusely that it rendered me anemic for years on end that blur my mind.

Somewhere between the ages of 45 and 50 (good memory), I had a period one month and none after that. No hot flashes, no nothing. I just started feeling better and better. As they say, you lose the "Baby Buggy", but keep the "Play Pen".

Lord give me chastity — but not yet.
Saint Augustine

Maureen

"Don't complain—change it.
If you can't change it—change the way you think about it."

Maya Angelou

i was always a fairly eclectic reader supporting my interests in Native American cultures, birds of prey, women in aviation, and artists/writers of New Mexico. Then the forays into the genres of romance, mystery, and adventure novels for what I call "bus books" — quick reads for the half hour commute.

Then came a change -- *The Change*. My reading choices intentionally focused on books by and about women. In particular, strong women characters and how they deal with life. I was not obsessed, but truly drawn to read how other women viewed life and death and dealt with life's issues. At age 49, I had successfully battled colon cancer with the strong support of my husband and women friends. At age 51, menopause seemed to warrant similar support.

What was this change all about? I recall at one point taking a picnic lunch out to Barr Lake State Park and spending a half day considering that question. Walking and watching birds, writing in my journal, and thinking, as an aggressive squirrel tried to steal my lunch! As we shared my peanut butter sandwich, I thought that this journey was comparatively better than some and worse than others I had been on. It was to be experienced at its fullest. However, it wasn't necessary to overreact. Half my life was over and this was to be a new beginning. So I walked back to the car, picking up a bird feather laying on the path as I went.

Seeing this as a learning experience, I began to read.

Strangely, I didn't read many books about menopause. My desire was to understand the lives of generations of women — their relationships to each other, their strengths and weaknesses. I had started a reading journal several years earlier. Here are my favorite authors and reading memories:

Books about Generations of Women:

Face of an Angel — Denise Chavez
Fried Green Tomatoes At the Whistle-Stop Cafe — Fannie Flagg
A Cure for Dreams — Kaye Gibbons
Charms for the Easy Life — Kaye Gibbons
A Mother and Two Daughters — Gail Godwin
Woman Warrior: Memoirs of a girlhood among ghosts — Maxine Hong Kingston
The Shell Seekers — Rosamunde Pilcher
Colony — Anne Rivers Siddons
The Kitchen God's Wife — Amy Tan

Women Dealing with Life:

And the Desert Shall Blossom — Phyllis Barber
Having Our Say: The Delany Sister's first 100 years — Sadie and Bessie Delany
Father Melancholy's Daughter — Gail Godwin
Solar Storms — Linda Hogan
Cowboys Are My Weakness — Pam Houston
The Steep Ascent — Anne Morrow Lindbergh
Refuge — Terry Tempest Williams

Stories With Strong Female Characters:

Cat's Eye — Margaret Atwood
The Pull of the Moon — Elizabeth Berg
Rubyfruit Jungle — Rita Mae Brown
The Solace of Open Spaces — Gretel Erlich
Windbreak: Woman Rancher on the Northern Plains — Linda Hasselstrom
The Bean Trees — Barbara Kingsolver
Pigs in Heaven — Barbara Kingsolver

Darion

*O*ur mother's generation took a vow of silence about many aspects of the female experience, including the "change." This silence lasted for decades as women navigated their solitary way through menopause. Now there is movement toward bringing this experience out into small communities of women where we can share laughter, resources, sorrows, gifts and mysteries that emerge for us as we enter the second half of life.

You need to claim the events of your life to make yourself yours.
Anne-Wilson Schaef

Stephanie

*a*t first I thought I didn't have anything to say, but I do. I can't be the only woman to travel two new journeys at the same time, each affecting the other to a large degree. You see, I lost my daughter to leukemia at the same time I was beginning menopause. The emotional upheaval of grief and menopause was and continues to be tough.

On the other hand, the lightness I experience is about how absolutely wonderful it will be to get through this. And I have begun to explore things I've always wanted to do or try. I have the time, now, to spend on myself and I'm loving all of it. It reminds me of the poem, "When I Am an Old Woman I Shall Wear Purple..."

Life shrinks or expands in proportion to one's courage.
Anais Nin

Wayne

*a*t age 79 when he heard that his daughter and daughter-in-law were hot flashing and coming into menopause, he said, "Oh, I've already been through that!"

"No, It's not hot in here..."
Dick Roth

Barbara

*i*think a sex change operation is the way to go through menopause.

Just when I found out the meaning of life, they changed it.
George Carlin

Terri

No More Eggs

*i*t is now my 49th summer, two years into the changes I wrote about in the introduction to this book. I can now tell you it is possible to end up in the emergency room from this menopause stuff. But my little spell was a blessing in disguise, for I was forced to face reality.

One Saturday morning in June I had a garage sale and found myself sitting in my lawn chair out in the driveway sipping coffee and soaking up the late morning sun. It was warm, not extraordinarily hot. It had been a good day of releasing remnants of my past, passing former treasures on to their next owners. My old bedspread, an extra washer and dryer, a futon frame, white elephant Christmas presents that had outlived their rightful places in my heart and home. Dusty artifacts from another time. The good stuff was almost gone, so I closed up shop and called it a day.

Steve invited me to go on errands with him, just a little ride downtown to the mail box, dry cleaner, and bank. A hurried trip with no dillydallying around, since everything closed by one o'clock. I ran upstairs to lock the door and in my haste didn't bother with my purse. Off we went.

Although I'd eaten a quick bowl of cereal between customers, I was so hungry. Several times during the week I'd been struck with the shakes and mean sweats, once while out walking. It was just something going on with my body, telling me to eat. I told Steve that I'd probably need some lunch pretty soon. I was starving!

We pulled around the corner to park in front of the dry cleaners when I broke into a fiendish sweat and felt terribly sick. I asked him to stop the car and run into the drug store to get me some orange juice, quick! He purchased the juice and delivered it to this pathetic noodle. My hands were shaking so badly that I couldn't open the bottle. With his help, I sipped along and felt worse. He took one look at my gray, clammy face and said, "I'm taking you to the emergency room." Of course, I said, "No, I'm better, I'm just so hot and hungry." Then I said "I'll never speak to you again if you take me to the hospital!"

He drove cautiously along toward home, never mind the errands. While sitting at a stoplight, I folded. My heart was racing and a rapid pulse was pounding in my neck and behind my eyes. I said, "Take me to the hospital, I think I'm dying." I remember nothing else except a very young, tall intern coming out to the car to help me through the Emergency entrance. The weakness was stunning, for I couldn't stand up or talk.

A young woman doctor placed me on a gurney in the only

room left, formerly a holding room for mental cases. When she closed the door behind her, it locked from the outside and we were trapped. She was being held hostage with a sweating, incoherent woman. Calmly she called security to unlock the door, all the while looking at me nervously. After we were released from our cell, I was asked a barrage of questions, tested for sugar diabetes, hypoglycemia, thyroid activity, and administered two EKG's in case I was having a heart attack. I had to pee in a cup, have blood drawn, and make sure I wasn't having more of those tiny little strokes I told you about earlier. Four and one half hours later, Dr. Watt came in to report the results of his afternoon's work on me.

"Well, do you know about hot and cold flashes? You're in fine shape, except that I'll bet your hormones are in a tizzy. You must see your regular doctor Monday and have an evaluation. I'm just an ER guy, but I'll bet this has been a hormonal incident and you need to see someone versed in treating menopause. Well, now, I really need to go, you see there's this guy down the hall, fluid around his heart, a very interesting case, not that you're not interesting!"

So, free at last, we came along home, wondering how a lovely summer afternoon could have evaporated so strangely. Feeling frustrated that we'd not accomplished much. Me feeling embarrassed at taking up space in the Emergency Room for the hot flash from hell!

Monday was the appointment with my own Dr. Hillary Browne. She listened politely to my Saturday saga; I just omitted the hormonal diagnosis. I was certain that she'd say she wanted to check my blood sugars. Instead she said, "Sounds like hormones hopping up and down. Let's do a blood test."

Thursday afternoon the nurse called to give me the results. "Terri, Doctor Browne asked me to call and let you know that you have no estrogen. This is menopause. And... there are no more eggs. You're all done." I yelp, "Let's have a party!" A "There are no more eggs party" to celebrate making it this far.

After I got off the phone, I walked to my mail box, pondering this news. How could I have no more eggs and not even know it? Instead of an uplifting little card from a friend amongst the usual bills and grocery ads, two lonely pieces of mail awaited. A *Victoria's Secret* sale catalog plastered with sexy young fertile models sporting the tiniest lace streamers draped strategically around youthful, standing-at-attention breasts and supple firm thighs. And my personal invitation to join AARP, along with a membership card to prove that I'm officially of that certain age!

So what's the blessing in all of this, you ask? That blast from the hormonal furnace helped me realize that I am well into this transition and there's no turning back. It means freedom from wondering if I'm truly sick. Freedom to say what's really on my mind. I'm paying attention to diet and exercise, for I want to be all I can be at 50, and 60, and for how ever long I'm in this body. This is it! No more condoms snapping on and off, no more paralyzing cramps, no more cramming Tampax into my suitcase every time I go on vacation. There's a lot to be said for flashing, and I don't mean wearing a trench coat and nothing else!

What do you do with 365 used condoms? Melt them down, make them into a tire, then say, "It was a very good year!"
Anonymous

Unknown

Journal of Humanistic Psychology
Written by an 85-year-old man who learned he was dying

*i*f I had my life to live over again, I'd try to make more mistakes next time. I wouldn't try to be so perfect. We all have perfection fetishes. What difference does it make if you let people know you are imperfect? They can identify with you then. Nobody can identify with perfection.

I would relax more. I'd limber up. I'd be sillier than I've been on this trip. In fact, I know very few things that I would take so seriously. I'd be crazier. I'd be less hygienic. Isn't that nice?

I'd take more chances, I'd swim more rivers, I'd watch more sunsets, I'd go more places I've never been to.

You see, I was one of those people who lived sensibly and sanely hour after hour and day after day. In fact, I'd try to have nothing but beautiful moments--moment by moment. In case you didn't know it, that's the stuff that life is made of. Only moments. Don't miss the now.

If I had it to do all over again, I'd start barefoot earlier in the spring and stay that way later in the fall. I'd ride more merry-go-rounds, I'd watch more sunrises, and I'd play with more children, if I had my life to live over again. But you see, I don't. Neither you nor I know what is beyond, but we do know what is here. This is God's gift to you, and how you use it is your gift to God.

How would the child that you were view the person you've become?
Calendar Wisdom

Bibliography

Every effort has been made to locate authors and copyright ownership of all material used in this book; however, repeated attempts to secure permissions warranted no response from certain publishers. Any additions or corrections to sources will be appreciated.

ARTICLE

"Menopause, The Challenge of the Change", Dr. Gwendolyn Goldsby Grant, Essence, June, 1998.

BOOKS

Andrews, Lynn V. *Woman at the Edge of Two Worlds*. New York, HarperCollins, 1994.

Angelou, Maya. *Wouldn't Take Nothing For My Journey Now*. New York, Random House, 1993.

Atwood, Margaret. *Cat's Eye*. New York, Doubleday, 1988.

Barber, Phyllis. *And the Desert Shall Blossom*. Salt Lake City, Signature Books, 1991.

Berg, Elizabeth. *The Pull of the Moon.* New York, Random House, Inc. 1996.

Berry, Carmen Renee & Traeder, Tamara. *Girlfriends, Enduring Ties.* Wildcat Canyon Press, 1995.

Bombeck, Erma. *All I Know About Animal Behavior I learned in A Loehmann's Dressing Room.* New York, HarperCollins, 1995.

Borysenko, Joan, Ph. D. *A Woman's Book of Life.* New York, Riverhead Books, G. P. Putnam's Sons, 1996.

Boston Women's Health Book Collective. *The New Bodies, Ourselves.* New York, Simon & Schuster, Inc. 1984.

Brown, H. Jackson. *Life's Little Instruction Book.* Nashville, TN. Rutledge Hill Press, Inc. 1991.

Brown, Rita Mae. *Rubyfruit Jungle.* New York City, Bantam Books, 1973.

Canfield, Jack; Hansen, Mark Victor; Hawthorne, Jennifer Read; Shimoff, Marci. *Chicken Soup for the Woman's Soul.* Deerfield Beach, FL. Health Communications, Inc. 1996.

Chavez, Denise. *Face of An Angel.* New York, Farrar, Straus, and Giroux, 1994.

Delany, Sarah and A. Elizabeth Delany. *Having our say: the Delany sisters' first 100 years.* New York, Kodansha International, 1993.

Ehrlich, Gretel. *The Solace of Open Spaces.* New York, Viking, 1985.

Flagg, Fannie. *Fried Green Tomatoes at the Whistle-Stop Cafe.* New York, Random House, 1987.

Freedman, Rita. *Age Before Beauty.* White Plains, NY. Peter Pauper Press, Inc. 1991.

Gibbons, Kaye. *A Cure for Dreams.* Chapel Hill, NC. Algonquin Books, 1991.

Gibbons, Kaye. *Charms for the Easy Life.* New York, Putnam, 1993.

Godwin, Gail. *A Mother and Two Daughters.* New York, Viking Press, 1982.

Godwin, Gail. *Father Melancholy's Daughter.* New York, Morrow, 1991.

Greer, Germaine. *Women, Aging and the Menopause.* New York, Knopf, 1991.

Hasselstrom, Linda. *Windbreak: A Woman Rancher on the Northern Plains.* Berkeley, CA. Barn Owl Books, 1987.

Hayward, Susan. *A Guide for the Advanced Soul.* Crows Nest, Australia, In-Tune Books, 1985.

Hogan, Linda. *Solar Storms.* New York, Scribner, 1995.

Houston, Pam. *Cowboys Are My Weakness.* New York, WW Norton, 1992.

James, Sibyl. *The Adventures of Stout Mama.* Freedom, CA. Papier-Mache Press, 1993.

Kingsolver, Barbara. *The Bean Trees.* New York, Harper & Row, 1988.

Kingsolver, Barbara. *Pigs in Heaven.* New York, HarperCollins, 1993.

Kingston, Maxine Hong. *Woman Warrior: Memoirs of a girlhood among ghosts.* New York, Knopf, 1976.

Lindberg, Anne Morrow. *The Steep Ascent.* New York, Harcourt, Brace and Company, 1944.

Norris, Kathleen. *Dakota: A Spiritual Geography.* New York. Ticknor & Fields, 1993.

Pilcher, Rosamunde. *The Shell Seekers.* New York. St. Martin's Press, 1987.

Radner, Gilda. *It's Always Something.* Sydney & New York, Simon and Schuster, 1989.

Ross, Pat. *Menopause Madness, An Emphatic Little Book.* New York, Fireside, 1998.

Roth, Dick. *No, It's Not Hot in Here: A Husband's Guide to Understanding Menopause.* Georgetown, MA. Ant Hill Press/North Star Publications, 1999.

Sacks, Martha. *MENOPAWS (The Silent Meow).* Berkeley, CA. Ten Speed Press, 1995.

Sand, G. *Is It Hot In Here Or Is It Me?* New York, HarperCollins, 1993.

Sheehy, Gail. *The Silent Passage.* New York, Random House, 1992.

Siddons, Anne Rivers. *Colony.* New York, Harper Paperbacks, 1992.

Tan, Amy. *The Kitchen God's Wife.* New York, Putnam, 1991.

Utian, Wulf H. & Jacobowitz, Ruth S. *Managing Your Menopause.* Upper Saddle River, NJ, Prentice Hall, 1990.

Wholey, Dennis. *The Miracle of Change.* New York, Simon & Schuster, Inc. 1997.

Williams, Terry Tempest. *Refuge.* New York, Random House, Inc. 1991.

Calendar

At A Glance Timepeace Calendars, 1-888-424-8463.

Catalog

As We Change. A Marketplace for Women. Contains range of products for pre- and post-menopausal women who have an interest in the transition. 1-800-203-5585. www.aswechange.com

Comic Strip

For Better Or For Worse © Lynn Johnston Productions, Inc./Dist. by United Feature Syndicate, Inc.

Newsletter

Transitions for Women, Natural Solutions. Portland, OR, 1998. www.transitions-for-women.com

Patterns

Angel Goddess Dolls by
Lisa Hertzi, ©1995.
www.creativapress.com

What Do You Think?

Do you have a quotation, story, poem, memory, anecdote, or thought you'd like to share about the positives of entering, experiencing, or surviving this important time of life?

Send your contributions to:

More Menopause Pink/Creativa Press
2525 Arapahoe Ave., E4 - PMB 548
Boulder, CO 80302
or e-mail: tlmaskh@aol.com
www.creativapress.com

Include your name, source, and permission to publish so that you and the author will be correctly credited in Volume 2.

Thank you for your support.

Terri Malucci

Terri Malucci lives in Boulder, Colorado, near family, friends and next door to her significant other. She decided to write her "letter to the world" after discovering that not many other authors had found humor in menopause. In between hot flashes she captured a compendium of words designed to inspire and encourage her mid-life sisters through their own transitions. She loves traveling the world, listening to music, baking biscotti, cooking and writing, and drinking beer with ice from delicate china tea cups.

Li Hertzi is an artist, designer, computer adventurer, doll maker, and most recently teacher—online! She studied painting and illustration in New York City, and has shown her work throughout the United States. Her designs were featured on apparel for the last U.S.A. Olympic Cycling Team as well as many other team and bicycle shop garments. To learn more about her dolls and design work, visit www. creativapress.com.

Order Form

To order additional copies of
Menopause Pink, complete this information:

Ship to: (Please Print)

Name _____

Address _____

City _____ State _____ Zip _____

Phone _____

_____ Copies of *Menopause Pink* @ $9.95 ea $_____

Postage & Handling @ $2.50 per book $_____

Colorado residents add 3.8% tax $_____

Total Amount Enclosed $_____

Make checks payable to Creativa Press

creativa
press

2525 Arapahoe Ave. E4—PMB 548
Boulder, CO 80302
1-800-484-2308-PIN 8088

What others have to say about Menopause Pink

"A must read for every woman entering menopause—humor truly is the best medicine."

—Hillary Browne, M.D.

"*Menopause Pink* offers a delightful, insightful collection of anecdotes in the words of women who have 'been there, done that and gotten the t-shirt'—pearls of wisdom to pass along to anyone beginning her journey into second adulthood!"

—Janice Blanchard, MSPH, Older Women's Wellness

"Terri Malucci speaks from the heart. Her vision, candor and humor lead you laughing along a new journey of self-discovery."

—Dr. Frank Sabatino, Health Spa Physician

"Enough about hormone replacement! Now I know I'm not losing my mind along with my waistline."

—Maureen Crocker, Librarian

Terri Malucci decided to write her "letter to the world" after discovering that not many authors had found humor in menopause. In between hot flashes she captured a compendium of words designed to inspire and encourage her mid-life sisters through their own transitions.

creativa
press

Boulder, Colorado
©2000 Terri Malucci

ISBN 0-9673744-4-8

$9.95 U.S.A.
$14.95 Canada

9 780967 374444

50995